A Bite of Cheese

by Lucy Floyd
illustrations by Franklin Ayers

Harcourt Brace & Company

Orlando Atlanta Austin Boston San Francisco Chicago Dallas New York Toronto London

Fox said to Sheep, "I need a meal, Sheep. I might have to eat you."

"Please don't eat me," Sheep
pleaded.

"I might, I might not," Fox
teased.

"Eat bright green beans from my vine," Sheep said with pride. "Dine on cream, beets, wheat, and sweet ripe peaches."

"No deal," Fox whined.
"I don't like beans, cream,
beets, wheat, or peaches."

"Cheese?" Sheep asked. "For a treat?"

"I like cheese," Fox said. "Cheese seems like a fine treat, Sheep."

"Here's a neat game," Sheep said. "Let's each bite on the cheese. We'll see who gets it."

Fox smiled with glee.
"Tee-hee! With my teeth, I'll
win with ease! My prize will
be the cheese—and Sheep!"

"If I win," Sheep said with a wise smile, "you must not eat me."

"Right, right," Fox said. "Let me bite into that cheese!"

"All set?" Sheep asked.
Fox was dreaming of his
feast.

"You bet!" Fox yelled—and dropped the cheese!

"I win! The cheese is mine!" Sheep said.

"What a mean trick!" Fox whined. "Let me have a bite at least!"

"I might, I might not," Sheep teased.